MONTANA
AF413878

MONTANA'S NATIONAL BISON RANGE 1933
BIG MEDICINE, A RARE WHITE BISON, WAS HAILED AS A SYMBOL OF GOOD FORTUNE by THE SALISH AND KOOTENAI
1

U.S. NUCLEAR MISSILE SILOS
IN SPARSELY POPULATED areas like MONTANA PROTECT POPULATED URBAN REGIONS BY BEING A PRIMARY TARGET DURING AN ATTACK.
USA
2

MONTANANS HAVE the
3RD SHORTEST COMMUTE in
the U.S. WITH AN AVERAGE
TRAVEL TIME to WORK
OF 17.9 MINUTES.
3

IN 1981 the BILLINGS, MONTANA MAYOR OFFICIATED A o° + CLOWN WEDDING at A STORE CALLED CLOWN TOWN. +

TOBY TWIST ♡ twinkles

MONTANA WRITER

WILLIAM KITTREDGE COINED the PHRASE [THE LAST BEST PLACE] in HIS 1988 ANTHOLOGY, AND is CREDITED with POPULARIZING IT.

MALTA, MONTANA'S NAME ORIGIN

A GREAT NORTHERN OFFICIAL RANDOMLY CHOSE THE ~~the~~ NAME AFTER HIS FINGER LANDED ON THE ISLAND OF MALTA WHILE SPINNING A GLOBE.

AROUND 75% OF WILDFIRES IN MONTANA ARE REPORTEDLY CAUSED BY HUMANS.

SHEP A DEVOTED HERDING DOG, REMAINED at the FORT BENTON, MONTANA RAILWAY STATION FOR 5 YEARS, ANTICIPATING his DECEASED OWNER'S RETURN, UNTIL HIS OWN DEATH in 1941.
SHEP
8

UNLIKE MOST U.S. STATES, MONTANA REQUIRES EMPLOYERS TO HAVE A VALID REASON TO TERMINATE EMPLOYEES, MAKING FIRING MORE CHALLENGING.

9

AS OF 2019 local AND FORMER RESIDENTS OF BIG SANDY, MONTANA HAVE WORKED TO ESTABLISH the 'PUDDLE' A RECURRING PUDDLE ON MAIN STREET as A LOCAL LANDMARK.

ACCORDING TO A 2020 RELIGIOUS CENSUS
MONTANA RANKS 47 in the U.S. FOR ACTIVE FORMAL FAITH MEMBERSHIP.

11

THE CLOSURE OF THE OLD MONTANA STATE PRISON RESULTED FROM INHUMANE CONDITIONS + RIOTS.

THE Hi-LINE
is a NORTHERN MONTANA
REGION NAMED AFTER the RAIL-
ROAD TRACK RUNNING THROUGH IT.
13

IN 1944, A U.S. BOMBER DROPPED 350LB BOMBS ON THE YELLOWSTONE RIVER IN MILES CITY, MONTANA, TO BREAK UP AN ICE JAM.

14

THE USS MONTANA SUBMARINE HAS MONTANA-THEMED ROOMS AND A CREW MESS HALL WITH A GLACIER PARK PANORAMA.

15

MONTANA'S TALLEST BUILDING STANDS AT 22% THE SIZE OF THE HEIGHT OF THE EMPIRE STATE BUILDING.
EMPIRE STATE BUILDING
1250 FEET TALL
FIRST INTERSTATE CENTER
272 FEET TALL
*AS OF 2023

MONTANA'S OPEN RANGE LAW ALLOWS LIVE-STOCK TO ROAM FREELY ON UNFENCED ROADS.

MONTANA HAS NO SALES TAX, BUT COMPENSATES THROUGH A HIGH INCOME TAX RATE.
18

HELENA, MONTANA'S CAPITOL BUILDING HAD ITS COPPER DOME PAINTED WITH ALUMINUM PAINT IN 1933, BUT THE RESULT WAS SO UGLY IT WAS REFERRED TO AS A COOKING POT.

19

THE WORLD'S FIRST
~RECORDED~
T-REX FOSSIL
WAS FOUND NEAR
JORDAN,
MONTANA,
in 1802.

MAGGIE SMiTH HATHAWAY, NICKNAMED "the WHiRL-WiND" WAS ONE OF THE FIRST WOMEN ELECTED to THE MONTANA STATE LEGISLATURE in 1916. SHE DEDICATED HERSELF to WOMEN'S RIGHTS, CHILD WELFARE AND EDUCATION.

21

ZOMBIE APOCALYPSE

in 2013, HACKERS BROKE into a GREAT FALLS, montana T.V. STATION AND AIRED THE MESSAGE:

NATIVE FRESHWATER MUSSELS in MONTANA
4 INCHES
WESTERN PEARLSHELL
FOUND IN WESTERN RIVERS + STREAMS.
FATMUCKET
GIANT FLOATER
6 INCHES
6 INCHES
BOTH FOUND in EASTERN RIVERS.

23

THE HANGING tree 1865-1870

A TALL, DEAD PONDEROSA PINE in HELENA, MONTANA WAS USED TO HANG 10 "OUTLAWS." it WAS CUT DOWN in 1875 BY A METHODIST MINISTER WHO thought IT WAS A THREAT to THE ROOF OF HIS BARN.

24

THERE ARE AT LEAST 115 NAMED ISLANDS IN MONTANA.
SOURDOUGH ISLAND
COW ISLAND
WILD HORSE ISLAND

25

the BEARTOOTH HIGH-WAY, A SECTION OF ROAD BETWEEN RED LODGE, MONTANA + YELLOWSTONE, HAS BEEN CALLED 'the MOST BEAUTIFUL DRIVE IN AMERICA'.

26

IN the SUMMER OF 1976, CARDINAL AND FUTURE POPE ST. JOHN PAUL II VISITED his FRIEND, celebrated MASS, AND ATTENDED a POT-LUCK in GEYSER, MONTANA.

MONTANA
IS ONE OF TWO U.S. STATES WITHOUT DISTRACTED DRIVER LAWS.
28

MONTANA'S OLDEST PERSON
WALTER BREUNING lived to be 114 YEARS OLD. AND AT THE TIME OF HIS DEATH WAS THE OLDEST LIVING HUMAN.

29

RINGDOCUS

in 1886, A MORMON SETTLER KILLED A WOLF like CREATURE WITH A HYENA-SLOPING BACK NEAR ENNIS, MONTANA. the UNIDENTIFIED ANIMAL WAS TAXIDERMIED AND DISPLAYED at the "MADISON VALLEY HISTORY MUSEUM" YEARS later.

THE U.S. INDUSTRY STANDARD FOR MILK REQUIRES A SELL BY DATE OF 24 DAYS AFTER IT'S PASTEURIZED, IN MONTANA IT'S 12 DAYS.

40% of U.S. COAL
COMES FROM the POWDER
RIVER BASIN, A 120 MILE
STRIP OF LAND ON THE
MONTANA + WYOMING
BORDER.

MONTANA HAS AT LEAST 86 hillSIDE LETTERS THROUGHOUT the STATE.

33

1989 HELENA MONTANA TRAIN WRECK FACTS

OCCURRED AT 4:38AM IN -30°F TEMPERATURES.

0 HUMAN CASUALTIES.

EXPLOSION CAUSED BY IMPACTED CHEMICALS.

DAMAGED BUILDINGS AND CUT CITY POWER.

SOME ROCK FORMATIONS in MONTANA APPEAR TO BE ARRANGED by HUMANS, BUT ARE ACTUALLY the RESULT OF NATURAL PROCESSES.

MONTANA IS THE 1ST STATE TO APPROVE A BILL THAT BANS TIKTOK, A SOCIAL MEDIA PLATFORM SUSPECTED OF SPYING FOR A FOREIGN GOVERNMENT.

36

18% OF MONTANA'S town PLACE NAMES ARE named AFTER PHYSICAL FEATURES IN THE LAND.

GLACIER

BIG TIMBER

GREAT FALLS

37

IN 1985, FRAGMENTS FROM MONTANA'S STATE DINOSAUR the MAIASAURA, BECAME THE 1ST DINOSAUR TO JOURNEY into SPACE.

MONTANA is THE SISTER STATE OF JAPAN'S KUMAMOTO PREFECTURE.

A SISTER STATE RELATIONSHIP IS A long-TERM PARTNERSHIP BETWEEN TWO COMMUNITIES in TWO COUNTRIES.

IN 2009, the HELENA MONTANA POLICE DEPT. BOUGHT AN ISRAELI BOMB SNIFFING DOG WHO ONLY UNDERSTOOD COMMANDS IN HEBREW. A RABBI HELPED WITH WORD PRONUNCIATION.
40

TOMANOWOS

THE LARGEST FOUND METEOR in NORTH AMERICA is BELIEVED to HAVE LANDED in MONTANA, ~15,000 YEARS AGO.

41

PRINCIPAL MERIDIAN

THE INITIAL POINT SET in 1867, to MEASURE ALL OF MONTANA is ON A NAMELESS HILL in THE SOUTHWESTERN PART OF the STATE.

THE 7 MILE long
FLATHEAD TUNNEL
near TREGO, MONTANA
IS the 2ND
LONGEST RAILROAD
TUNNEL in
THE U.S.
ELK MOUNTAIN

43

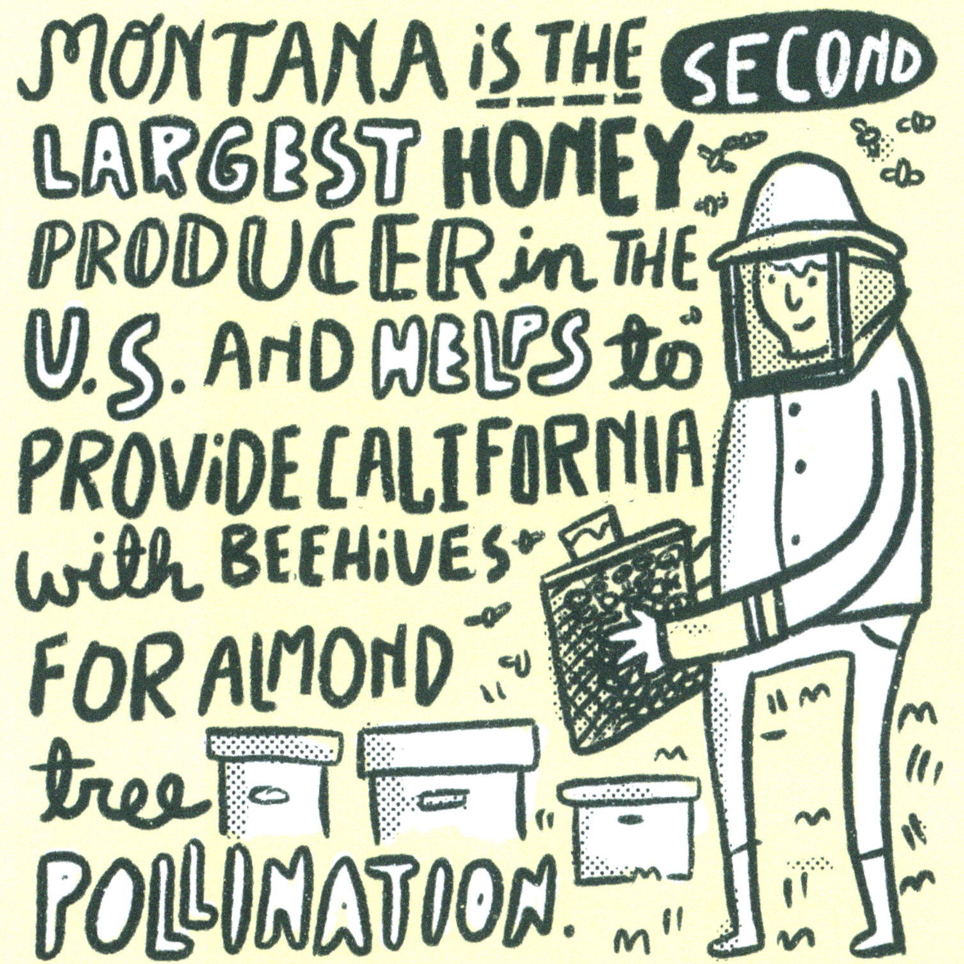
MONTANA IS THE SECOND LARGEST HONEY PRODUCER in THE U.S. AND HELPS to PROVIDE CALIFORNIA with BEEHIVES FOR ALMOND tree POLLINATION.
44

in 2018 PATRICIA SPONHEIM "PIANO PAT" RECEIVED THE SPIRIT OF MONTANA award for ENTERTAINING COUNTLESS PATRONS FOR 50+ YEARS at the SIP N' DIP TIKI LOUNGE in GREAT FALLS, MONTANA.

45

A FERAL DOG lived ON THE PROPERTIES AROUND THE BERKELEY PIT iN BUTTE, MONTANA. MiNE EMPLOYEES PROVIDED the DOG WITH FOOD, WATER AND SHELTER.

in 2019 LAWMAKERS PROPOSED COMPENSATION FOR MONTANANS EXPOSED to REGIONAL NUCLEAR TESTING FALLOUT.

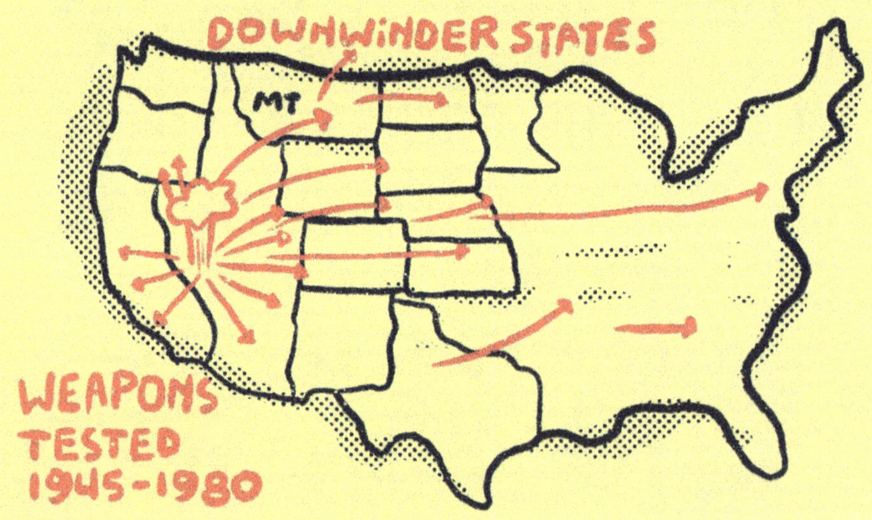

47

ACCORDING to A 2022 STUDY FROM HiGHSPEEDINTERNET.com, MONTANA HAS the SECOND SLOWEST INTERNET SPEED in the U.S...
48

FOUNDED iN 1936 NEAR NEIHART,
KiNG'S HiLL, NOW SHOWDOWN, iS montana's 1ST ski AREA.
49

BEFORE BECOMING A COUNTRY MUSIC legend CHARLEY PRIDE
PLAYED SEMI PRO BASEBALL in MONTANA FOR the EAST HELENA SMELTERITES.

FEBRUARY 1, 2023

A CHINESE SURVEILLANCE BALLOON WAS SPOTTED ABOVE BILLINGS, MONTANA, MAKING ITS WAY toward THE ATLANTIC OCEAN AND SHOT DOWN BY U.S. AUTHORITIES FOR INVESTIGATION.

51

SARAH GAMMON BROWN BICKFORD
A FORMER SLAVE WHO MOVED to MONTANA DURING the GOLD RUSH, SHE BECAME sole OWNER OF THE VIRGINIA CITY WATER CO. AND the 1ST BLACK WOMAN IN THE U.S. TO OWN A PUBLIC UTILITY.
SARAH'S OFFICE

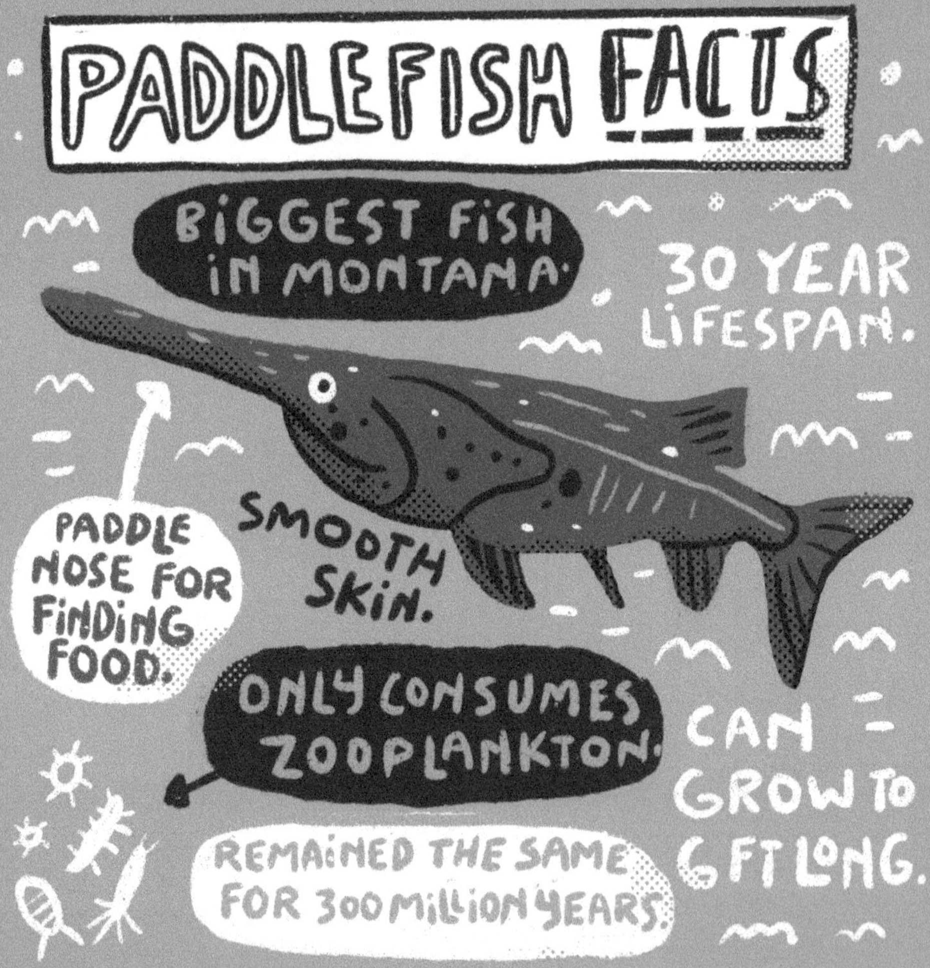

PADDLEFISH FACTS
BIGGEST FISH IN MONTANA.
30 YEAR LIFESPAN.
PADDLE NOSE FOR FINDING FOOD.
SMOOTH SKIN.
ONLY CONSUMES ZOOPLANKTON.
CAN GROW TO 6 FT LONG.
REMAINED THE SAME FOR 300 MILLION YEARS.
53

THE ONLY SPIDER
in MONTANA POISONOUS ENOUGH TO HARM
A HUMAN is THE BLACK WIDOW. 
BITES ARE VERY RARE.
54

MONTANA STACK FACTS

BLACK EAGLE
SMOKE
STACK

GREAT FALLS
MONTANA

506 FT
TALL

IN OPERATION
1893–1980

DEMOLISHED
1982

the BIG
STACK

ANACONDA
MONTANA

585 FT
TALL

IN OPERATION
1919–1980

REMAONS
STANDING

55

MONTANA
WAS the FIRST
STATE TO
LEGALIZE
VIDEO
GAMBLING.*
*ALWAYS LEGAL IN NEW
JERSEY AND NEVADA.
56

THOUGH RAISED IN OTHER STATES FILM DIRECTOR DAVID LYNCH HAS REFERRED TO HIMSELF AS:
JUST A GUY FROM MISSOULA, MONTANA.

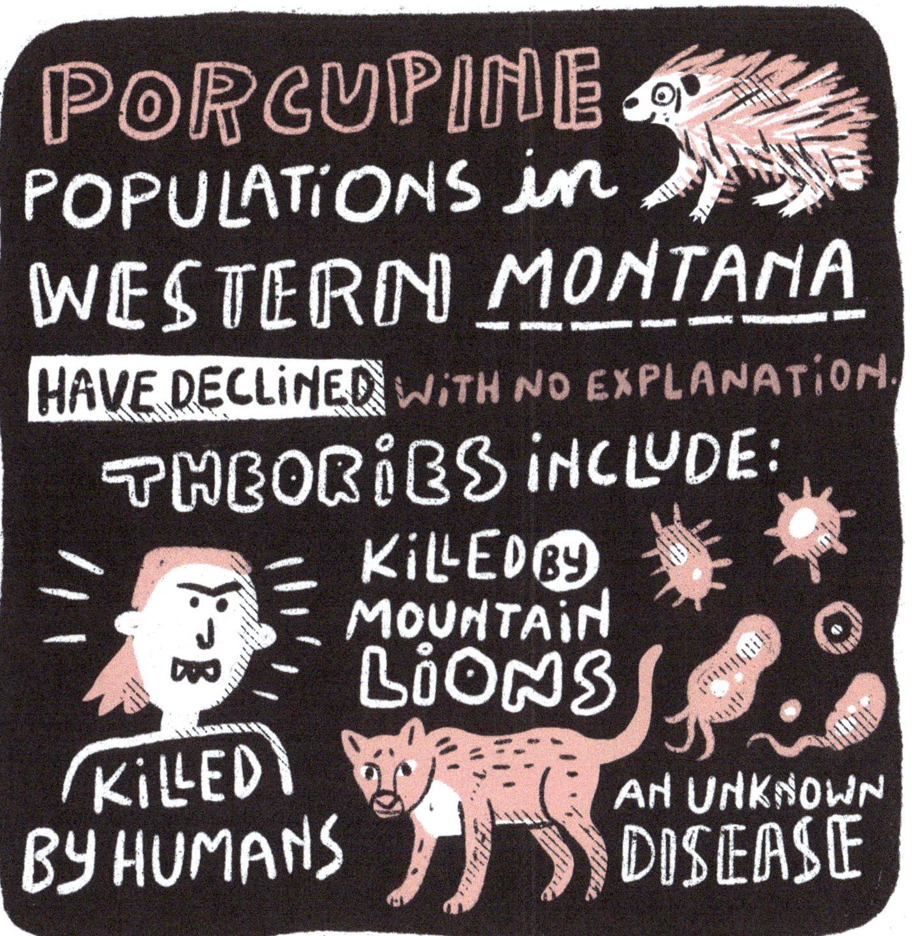

PORCUPINE
POPULATIONS in
WESTERN MONTANA
HAVE DECLINED WITH NO EXPLANATION.
THEORIES INCLUDE:
KILLED BY MOUNTAIN LIONS
KILLED BY HUMANS
AN UNKNOWN DISEASE

DR. LEROY HOOD, ORIGINALLY FROM MISSOULA, MONTANA WAS INSTRUMENTAL in DEVELOPING the FIRST AUTOMATED DNA SEQUENCER.

THE SEQUENCER WAS USED TO MAP THE FULL HUMAN GENOME, A PROJECT WHICH HAS HELPED IN THE UNDERSTANDING OF DISEASE AND HUMAN EVOLUTION.

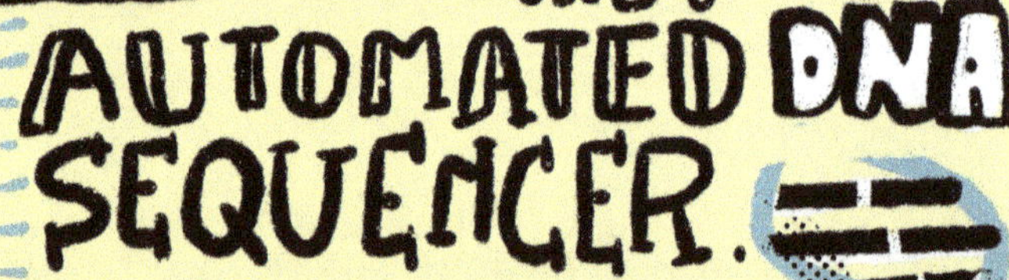

ACCORDING TO THE 2021 U.S. CENSUS, THE MEDIAN AGE in MONTANA is 40.1 YEARS.

CANADA AND MONTANA SHARE 545 MILES of BORDER, 14 BORDER CROSSINGS AND AN INTERNATIONAL PEACE PARK.

THE PARENTS OF **LEGENDARY** SKATEBOARDER **TONY HAWK** → WERE FROM **BILLINGS, MONTANA.**

SUSIE **WALKING BEAR** YELLOWTAIL

GRANDMOTHER OF AMERICAN INDIAN NURSES

FROM PRYOR, MONTANA **WAS** the **FIRST** CROW AND ONE OF THE **FIRST NATIVE** AMERICAN NURSES in the UNITED STATES.

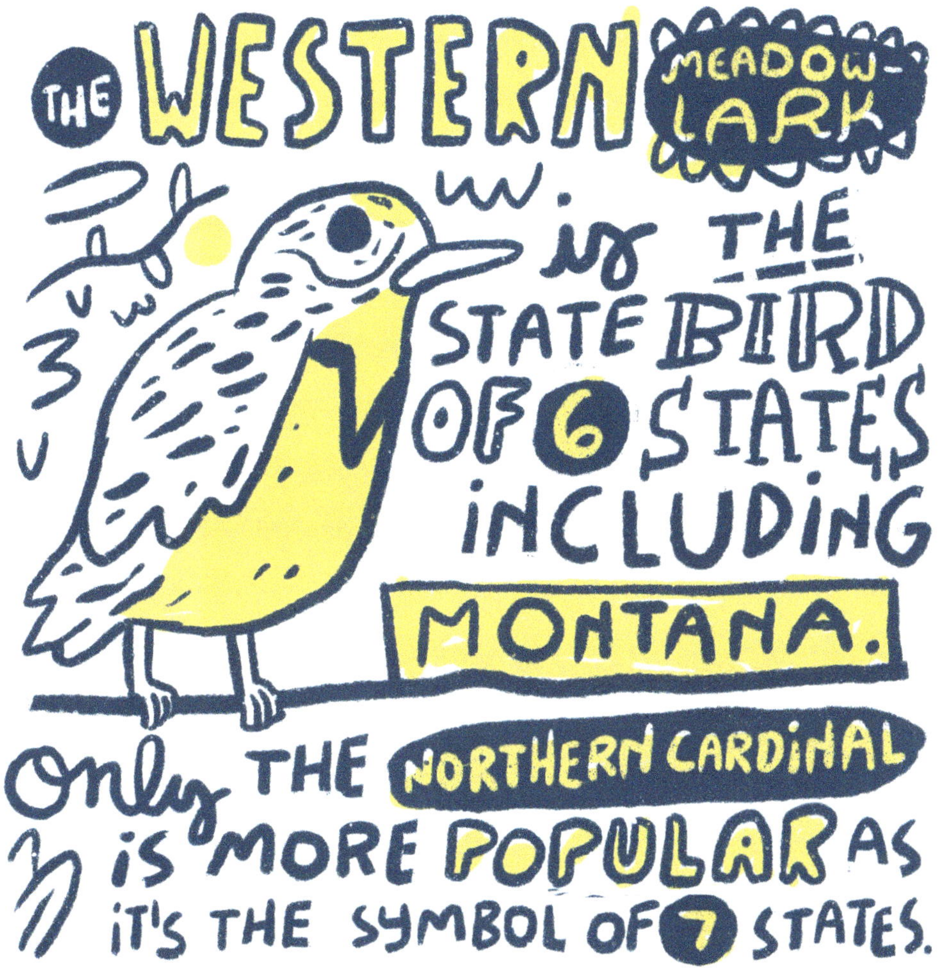

THE WESTERN MEADOWLARK
is THE STATE BIRD OF 6 STATES INCLUDING MONTANA.
Only THE NORTHERN CARDINAL is MORE POPULAR AS it's THE SYMBOL OF 7 STATES.
64

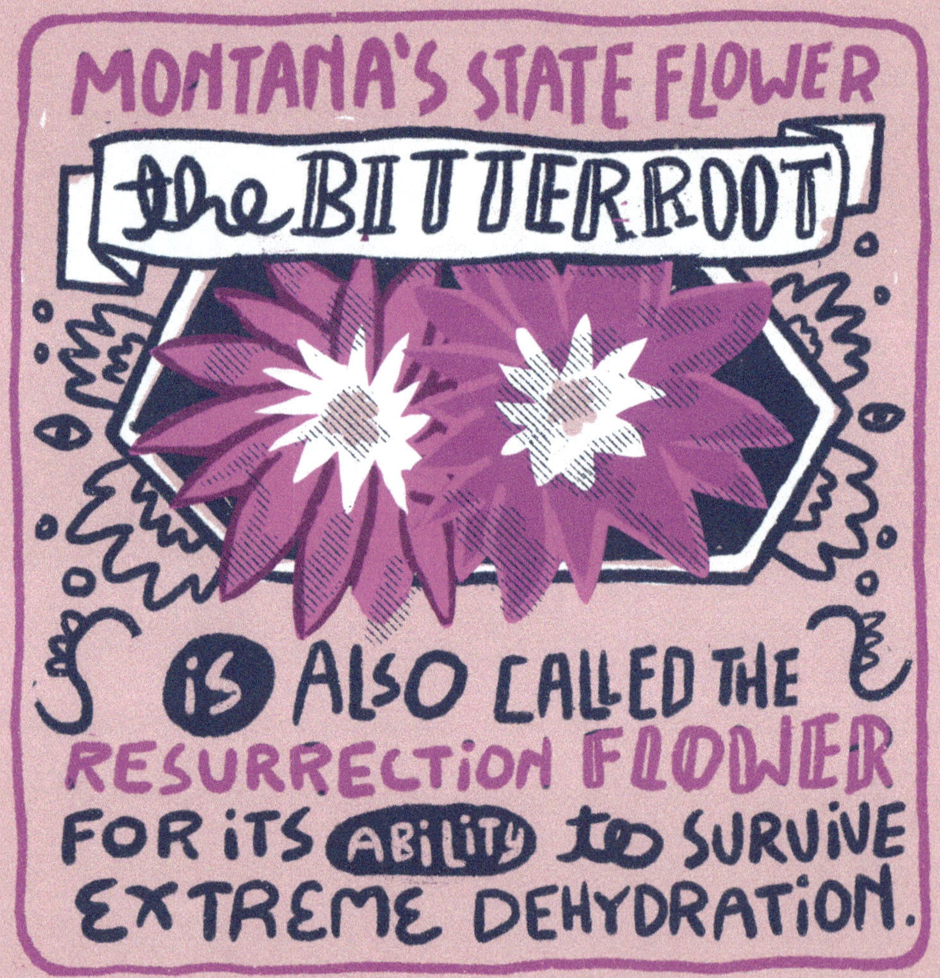

MONTANA'S STATE FLOWER
the BITTERROOT
IS ALSO CALLED THE
RESURRECTION FLOWER
FOR ITS ABILITY TO SURVIVE
EXTREME DEHYDRATION.
65

the PONDEROSA PINE

WAS CHOSEN as MONTANA'S STATE *tree* FOR ITS LUMBER PRODUCTION **AND** ABUNDANCE.

MONTANA'S TALLEST PONDEROSA PINE *is* **200+** FT *tall*, 3RD LARGEST in THE U.S. AND NICKNAMED ← 'BIG PINE'.

67

ORGANISMS that LIVE IN THE ACIDIC WATERS OF THE BERKELEY PIT in BUTTE, MONTANA ARE CALLED EXTREMOPHILES.

68

CEMETERY island

ON CANYON FERRY LAKE, MONTANA is THE ONLY VISIBLE REMAINS OF ITS TOWN BURIED BELOW the WATER.

HUTTERITES, A PACIFIST, BREAK-AWAY CHRISTIAN COMMUNITY PRODUCES 98% of MONTANA'S EGGS.

LEGEND has it, THE
MONTANA STATE SONG
WAS WRITTEN AND COMPOSED
in 30 MINUTES.
M·O·N·T·A·N·A
MONTANA,
I LOVE YOU
71

MONDAK MONTANA
WAS ONCE A THRIVING TOWN WHOSE ECONOMY WAS BASED ON SELLING ALCOHOL to NORTH DAKOTA in THE EARLY 1900's WHEN IT WAS PROHIBITED.
MT
ND

72

SNOWDEN BRIDGE
STANDS AS MONTANA'S SOLE VERTICAL lift BRIDGE, SERVING FOR OVER 70 YEARS. the LIFT WAS ONLY UTILIZED 16 TIMES DURING ITS OPERATION.

73

A MINE in SOUTHERN MONTANA is THE U.S.'s ONLY PRODUCER OF PALLADIUM, A RARE METAL USED in CARS to HELP CONTROL EXHAUST EMISSIONS.

74

HENRY PLUMMER'S GOLD

is the hidden treasure, left behind by the infamous sheriff of Bannack, Montana, after his death in 1864.

BRANDS ON ANIMALS
IS AN INDICATOR OF OWNERSHIP OF LIVESTOCK IN MONTANA AND A FAMILY HEIRLOOM.
FISH HOOK
TURKEY TRACK
TWO DOT
HAT X
N BAR
CIRCLE
FORTY
HOUR GLASS
AS OF 2011, OVER 55,000 BRANDS HAVE BEEN REGISTERED IN IN MONTANA.

MINNIE SPOTTED-WOLF, FROM HEART BUTTE, MONTANA WAS the 1ST NATIVE AMERICAN (BLACKFOOT TRIBE) WOMAN to ENLIST in THE U.S. MARINES.

the SKATING AMPHITHEATER 1883-1889
WAS A ROLLER SKATING RINK IN HELENA, MONTANA THAT HELD RACING CONTESTS, WALKING COMPETITIONS, + BICYCLE EXHIBITIONS.
78

THOUGH ONLY A MONTANAN for 3 YEARS FRANCIS THOMPSON PRODUCED the SKETCH FROM WHICH the STATE's SEAL is BASED UPON.
THE SEAL OF THE TERRITORY OF MONTANA
ORO Y PLATA
THE GREAT SEAL OF THE STATE OF MONTANA
ORO -Y- PLATA

79

ACCORDING to the CDC:
MONTANA is ONE of the MOST HEALTHY WEIGHT STATES in THE U.S..

MONTANA IS THE FIRST U.S. STATE TO APPROVE THE USAGE OF 3D PRINTED WALLS FOR CONSTRUCTION.

81

JUNKED CARS WERE ONCE used ON MONTANA RIVER BANKS to PREVENT EROSION.

MONTABAHN
DURING the 1990's, MONTANA HiGHWAY SPEED LIMITS WERE DEFINED as 'REASONABLE AND PRUDENT' RATHER THAN A STANDARD NUMBER.

THE TREASURE STATE
SPELLING BBB
FEATURES SPELLERS in GRADES
4-8 FROM ALMOST EVERY
COUNTY in MONTANA.
THE WINNER REPRESENTS MONTANA
AT the SCRIPPS NATIONAL SPELLING BEE.
84

PEKIN NOODLE PARLOR is the OLDEST CONTINUOUSLY OPERATED CHINESE RESTAURANT in the UNITED STATES AND is LOCATED in BUTTE, MONTANA.

MONTANA'S SOLE AREA CODE, 406, IS INCORPORATED INTO THE NAMES OF OVER 400 BUSINESSES BASED WITHIN THE STATE.

MENACE OF MONTANA

SPOTTED KNAPWEED IS FOUND IN EVERY COUNTY IN MONTANA. INFESTATIONS CAN BE CONTROLLED USING WEEVIL LARVAE→ TO EAT THE PLANT.

ACCORDING TO A FEDERAL SURVEY
47%
OF MONTANA
RESIDENTS
WERE born
IN MONTANA.
88

IN 1970's MONTANA, NUMEROUS MYSTERIOUS CATTLE MUTILATIONS WERE DISCOVERED.
SUSPECTS INCLUDE:
LIGHTNING
HIPPIE OCCULTISTS
DISEASE
ALIENS
89

"L. RON HUBBARD, FOUNDER OF SCIENTOLOGY, CONSIDERED HELENA, MONTANA HIS HOMETOWN, HAVING ATTENDED HIGH SCHOOL THERE.

MISSOULA, MONTANA'S FIRST INHABITANTS WERE SALISH TRIBE MEMBERS WHO NAMED THE AREA, NEMISSOOLATAKA MEANING "RIVER OF AMBUSH".

CONVICT Road

FROM 1910-25 PRISON labor BUILT over 230 MILES OF MOSTLY WESTERN MONTANA ROADS.

3 GUARDS
• CARRIED NO FIRE-ARMS
• HAD BLOOD HOUNDS + HORSES.

100 CONVICTS
• PAYED 50¢ PER DAY FOR FOOD
• 2 BATHS PER WEEK
• WORE PLAIN CLOTHES

92

TED KACZYNSKI'S 10'×12' CABIN in LINCOLN, MONTANA WAS SOLD at AUCTION in 2011 FOR $190K.
THE PROCEEDS WENT TO THE FAMILIES OF HIS VICTIMS.

CENTRAL MONTANA near GREAT FALLS
the 'BELT METEOR CRATER,'
A 100FT WIDE, 300FT DEEP
BOWL-SHAPED CAVITY is NOT
A RESULT OF CRASHING SPACE
MATTER BUT A SINKHOLE
FORMED by WATER EROSION.

94

ENFORCES A 'DARK SKY ORDINANCE,' MANDATING *light* FIXTURES to PREVENT UPWARD SHINING, CREATING A DARKER SKY for STARGAZING.

95

MONTANA'S HIGHWAY 200
is the LONGEST STATE HIGHWAY in the U.S.,
A 10 hour JOURNEY FROM END to END AT 70 MPH WITH NO STOPS.
96

AMONG the 5 AIRPORTS IN MONTANA WITH 'INTERNATIONAL' im THEIR TITLE ONLY 1 OPERATES INTERNATIONAL COMMERCIAL FLIGHTS.

97

THE NAME 'ANACONDA' IN ANACONDA MINING COMPANY, BUTTE, MONTANA, WAS INSPIRED BY A CIVIL WAR ANALOGY, LIKENING THE UNION ARMY TO AN ANACONDA SQUEEZING THE CONFEDERATE FORCES.

BETWEEN 1949-54 MOST buildings IN CANTON, MONTANA, WERE SUBMERGED below CANYON FERRY RESERVOIR w/the EXCEPTION OF ST. JOSEPH CHURCH WHICH was MOVED 2.5 MILES from its ORIGINAL site. The CHURCH REMAINS A HISTORICAL site + COMMUNITY CENTER.

in BYNUM, MONTANA, A BOW HUNTER BRAVELY FENDED OFF A BEAR ATTACK by USING A SURVIVAL TIP FROM his GRANDMA: SHOVING HIS ARM DOWN THE ANIMAL'S THROAT.
100

MONTANA BOASTS APPROXIMATELY 169,829 MILES OF RIVERS, WITH 388 MILES DESIGNATED as WILD AND scenic to SAFEGUARD their BEAUTY, CULTURAL SIGNIFICANCE AND OTHER CHERISHED VALUES.

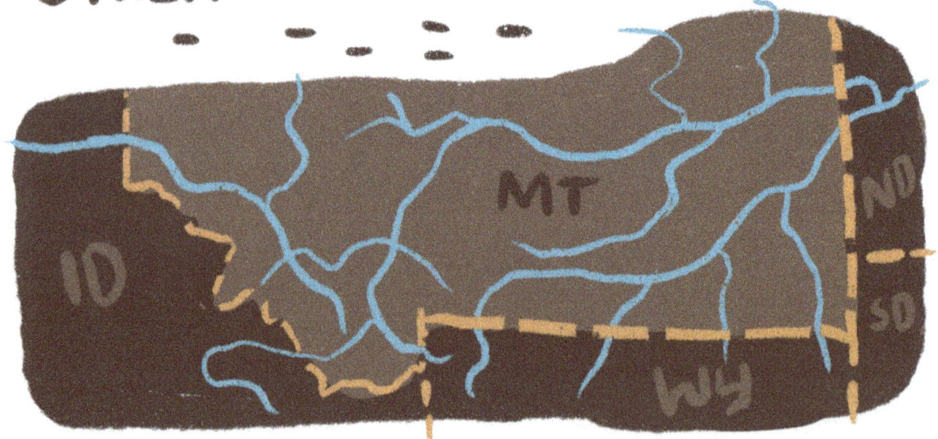

101

THE FLOOD OF 1964
STANDS AS MONTANA'S WORST RECORDED NATURAL DISASTER, AFFECTING 20% OF the STATE.
102

IF YOU like THIS BOOK TRY OTHER QUICK facts BOOKS, AVAILABLE AT THE COOLEST STORES OR QUICKFACTSBOOKS.com